COLONIAL PEOPLE

The Miller

CHRISTINE PETERSEN

Marshall Cavendish
Benchmark

New York

This publication represents the opinions and views of the author based on Christine Petersen's personal experience, knowledge, and
research. The information in this book serves as a general guide only. The author and publisher have used their best efforts in preparing
this book and disclaim liability rising directly and indirectly from the use and application of this book.

Other Marshall Cavendish Offices:

Marshall Cavendish International (Asia) Private Limited, 1 New Industrial Road, Singapore 536196 • Marshall Cavendish
International (Thailand) Co Ltd., 253 Asoke, 12th Flr, Sukhumvit 21 Road, Klongtoey Nua, Wattana, Bangkok 10110, Thailand •
Marshall Cavendish (Malaysia) Sdn Bhd, Times Subang, Lot 46, Subang Hi-Tech Industrial Park, Batu Tiga, 40000 Shah Alam,
Selangor Darul Ehsan, Malaysia

Marshall Cavendish is a trademark of Times Publishing Limited

All websites were available and accurate when this book was sent to press.

Library of Congress Cataloging-in-Publication Data

Petersen, Christine.
The miller / Christine Petersen.
p. cm. — (Colonial people)
Includes index.
Summary: "Explore the life of a colonial miller and his importance to the
community, as well as everyday life, responsibilities, and social practices
during that time"—Provided by publisher.
ISBN 978-1-60870-416-3 (print)
ISBN 978-1-60870-638-9 (ebook)
1. Millers—United States—History—17th century—Juvenile literature. 2.
Millers—United States—History—18th century—Juvenile literature. 3.
Mills and mill-work—United States—History—17th century—Juvenile
literature. 4. Mills and mill-work—United States—History—18th
century—Juvenile literature. 5. United States—History—Colonial period,
ca. 1600-1775—Juvenile literature. I. Title.
HD8039.M562U563 2012
664'.720097309033—dc22
2010033890

Editor: Joy Bean
Publisher: Michelle Bisson
Art Director: Anahid Hamparian
Series Designer: Kay Petronio

Expert Reader: Paul Douglas Newman, Ph.D., Department of History, University of Pittsburgh at Johnstown

Photo research by Marybeth Kavanagh

Cover photo by North Wind Picture Archives

The photographs in this book are used by permission and through the courtesy of: *North Wind Picture Archives*: 4, 7, 10, 12, 37, 40; Nancy
Carter: 16; *Getty Images*: SSPL, 13; Ed Nano, 34; *Corbis*: David Muench, 18; Derek Middleton/Frank Lane Picture Agency, 38; *The
Image Works*: SSPL, 23; *PhotoEdit, Inc.*: Cleo Photography, 26; *The Colonial Williamsburg Foundation*, 27; *The Bridgeman Art Library*: Private
Collection/© Look and Learn, 30

Printed in Malaysia (T)
1 3 5 6 4 2

CONTENTS

ONE

Life in a New Land

The promise of wealth drew English settlers to Jamestown, Virginia, in 1607. There were rumors that gold could be found in America. Wood and iron would be almost as valuable as gold if settlers could export it to England, for the English used large amounts of these materials to build ships. Colonists also hoped to find the Northwest Passage, which was a shortcut connecting the Atlantic and Pacific oceans that was rumored to exist. If located, this route would save ships a long trip around Africa or South America. It would also keep English ships safe from Spanish pirates.

The cost of creating a colony was high. English merchants worked together toward this goal. After getting permission

Colonists relied on food and other goods shipped from England to survive in their new home.

from King James I, they formed a business called the Virginia Company of London. The company began to raise money and to seek volunteers to make the journey to Virginia. They prepared a detailed plan to guide the settlers. Upon arriving, some of the men were supposed to build a walled fort to defend their houses. Others were to begin planting food so the group would be prepared for winter.

The settlers got their shelters up but then ran into trouble. None of them had been farmers in England. They found that the soil at Jamestown was soggy and salty. The few men who tried to plant gardens had no success. Most of the men didn't bother. Instead of working together to solve these problems, they went off to look for gold. Meanwhile, the food supplies they had brought from England began to dwindle. Local American Indians provided the colonists with some food for a while, but eventually the men had to fend for themselves. The situation would have become desperate if not for Captain John Smith.

Smith was a commoner, born to parents without wealth or social position. The gentlemen settlers did not like Smith's tendency to speak his mind. They were unhappy that the Virginia Company had selected him as one of its leaders. But Smith proved worthy of the company's trust.

When others were ready to give up, Smith set off to explore the region and to search for food. Algonquin Indian scouts captured Smith and brought him to their leader, Powhatan. The Indians held Smith captive for two months, until Powhatan ordered a frightening ritual. His men raised clubs over Smith's head as if they were going to beat him to death. At the last moment, Powhatan's young daughter, Pocahontas, ran up to the men. She threw herself over Smith to protect him. Powhatan stopped the ritual and eventually released Smith. The two men struck an agreement: Powhatan would have his men provide corn and meat to Jamestown in exchange for English goods, such as metal tools and clothing.

Captain John Smith became the new leader of the colony at Jamestown.

Smith's success brought praise from the other settlers, who elected him president. The new leader wasted no time before laying down a firm set of rules. Each settler was expected to do his part every day. "He who does not work," stated Smith, "will not eat."

Colonial Crops

It took several decades, but Jamestown colonists learned the skills needed to survive in their new home. Women and families joined the men who had established the colony. Jamestown grew steadily, and new communities formed around it. The colonists came from many backgrounds. There were gentlemen from wealthy English families, skilled **craftsmen**, poor people trying to escape London's miserable crowds, and even orphans. As Captain Smith had understood, the only thing these people had in common was the need to eat. Colonists became good hunters, bringing home deer and turkey meat. They began to use American Indian fishing nets and canoes to obtain fish and mussels. Flavorful berries and nuts were found in the forests. The Algonquins also introduced settlers to vegetables such as squash and beans, which could be grown in the garden.

Jamestown colonists were glad for these foods. But like all Europeans, they were used to having bread at every meal. European breads were made from the seeds of wheat, oats, barley, or rye that had been ground into flour. Colonists had brought these **grains** from England, but the plants did not produce enough seed when grown in Virginia soils. The settlers had better success with corn, which their Algonquin neighbors showed them how to farm. Corn flour, called **meal**, was heavier than the wheat flour colonists had cooked in England. It did not rise to produce airy bread, but it was flavorful and filling. Jamestown colonists soon enjoyed cornbread, pancake-like fried johnnycakes, and corn porridge as regular parts of their diet.

In the 1620s, new groups of English colonists settled the forested shores of Massachusetts Bay, north of Virginia. This region came to be known as New England. The settlers there were English Congregationalists, sometimes known as Pilgrims. Congregationalists sought to create private religious communities, separate from people of other faiths. Unlike Virginia's first colonists, they came to settle communities instead of seeking quick riches, and so they brought many experienced farmers.

Farming was not easy in New England. Settlers had to clear sections of forest to make room for fields. Then they had to remove rocks from the soil before they could plant crops. The Pilgrims suffered long winters, and each year there was only a short period

Colonists often ate meals such as this one, which consists of corn porridge and johnnycakes.

when crops could grow. Wheat tended to become moldy in the damp, cold New England climate. But farmers there were happy to find that they could grow rye as well as corn. They mixed the two grains to make a brown bread that was heavy and hearty.

Dutch colonists initially claimed the land between Virginia and New England. England took over their colony in 1664, but the region remained popular among colonists from different parts of Europe. The climate and soils there were perfect for farming. Settlers could raise wheat, oats, barley, rye, and corn. New York, New Jersey, Pennsylvania, and Delaware eventually became known as the breadbasket colonies. They **exported** large amounts of grain north to New England and south to southern colonies. Ships carried extra grain to other English colonies in the Caribbean Sea, where the grain fed millions of slaves working on sugar plantations.

What a Grind

Wherever it was produced, people could not make grain into bread until they ground it into flour or meal. At first, colonists had no option but to grind grains by hand with tools that had been invented centuries earlier. Nothing was simpler than the **mortar** and **pestle**. The mortar was a large stone or tree stump with a hole carved in the center. The pestle was carved from a thick stick. The technique was simple. The colonial farmer or his wife poured whole grains into the mortar and pounded them with the pestle until they broke into tiny, powdery fragments. Corn kernels were large and hard, so they were hard to break up. Colonists learned to soak them in water before grinding them. Even so, it could take hours to produce enough flour for a few meals.

Ancient Foods

The ancestors of wheat, barley, and rye grew in a region called the Fertile Crescent, around the Tigris and Euphrates rivers in present-day Iraq, Turkey, and Syria. Ancient people began to collect these wild grains more than 11,000 years ago. Eventually they chose the best-tasting and hardiest varieties to grow on farms.

Maize, or corn, is a grass. The oldest evidence of maize farming comes from Mesoamerica, around the southern edge of the Gulf of Mexico. Archaeologists have found corncobs that are more than seven thousand years old. The original maize plant is called teosinte. Its ears are much smaller than modern corncobs and contained only a few kernels. Ancient Mesoamericans bred teosinte to make larger kernels and to bear more seeds per cob. Maize cultivation spread until this grain was found across North and South America.

At one time people in South America raised three hundred types of corn, but American Indians mostly raised flint maize. This variety has a hard outer coating and a soft, fleshy interior. People cooked corncobs in the coals of a fire or crushed them as meal that could be cooked in many ways.

Maize was a popular crop for the colonists.

When they could, colonists replaced the mortar and pestle with a **quern**. The quern was made from two stones placed one atop the other. The stones were rounded on top and had a flat bottom. The bottom stone was fixed in place. In the middle of the top stone was a large hole allowing grain to fall. A second, smaller hole along its edge allowed the user to insert a wooden handle and rotate the top stone. Grain was crushed between the stones and pushed out the sides. Many querns were enclosed in wooden barrels or boxes, which caught the flour or meal as it fell.

Querns were used to grind grain to make flour.

Colonists didn't mind working hard, but they were glad for the opportunity to pass a time-consuming job to an expert. Every community hoped to attract a miller. His huge millstones powered by water or teams of animals were fast and powerful. They made flour and meal with a fine texture that cooked well and tasted delicious.

TWO

Plymouth Chooses a Miller

For several years after founding Plymouth Colony, the Pilgrims focused all their energy on survival. Like the settlers at Jamestown, they built homes and a meetinghouse in which to hold church services. Working with local American Indians, they planted corn and other crops. Fishermen sought out the best places to lay their nets and drop their lines along the coast. Town leaders sorted out the rules of their society.

By 1632 the community had established a rhythm, and it was time to consider bigger projects. Young Stephen Deane proposed a plan to the colony's leaders. He wanted to set up a **gristmill**. His gristmill would use a waterwheel to turn a pair of large grinding stones. Townspeople could bring their grain to the mill and have it ground quickly. Deane hoped to become Plymouth Colony's first miller.

The Miller's Toll

Leaders of Plymouth Colony knew that everyone could benefit from the mill, so they decided that the colony should help pay for its construction. They wanted to encourage Stephen Deane to stay in their community by making sure he was well paid. A legal order explained the terms of his work as Plymouth's miller:

> He should receive one pottle out of every bushel for toll and no more; and . . . in case the said Stephen can beat all the corn that is or shall be used in the colony, it shall not be lawful for any other to set up a work of that kind except it be for his own use, or freely . . . to give leave to others to make use of the same.

The order specified that Deane would be paid in grain. A **pottle** was a drinking bowl with a volume of 2 quarts (1.9 liters). The **bushel** had a capacity of 8 gallons (30 l), and each gallon holds 4 quarts (3.8 l). Deane therefore received one-sixteenth of all the grain he ground. This payment was called the miller's **toll**.

Deane's agreement with the leaders of Plymouth Colony was also created to try and keep him from cheating. He might have been an honest man, but millers were generally considered untrustworthy. This reputation began in England, where millers often worked for wealthy landowners. The lord built the mill and rented the miller use of the equipment. The miller ground all of the lord's grain and received a toll. The lord's farmer tenants could also come to the mill, but they had to pay a toll to both the miller and their lord. The English miller wound up with only a small portion of the grain he milled.

Bringing in the Harvest

Harvesttime meant hard work for everyone. Men, women, and children walked down each row of the cornfields. They used knives to cut large, mature ears of corn from the stalks. Then they left the ears to dry in **cribs**, wooden boxes raised on posts above the ground.

A common tool for harvesting wheat and other grains was the L-shaped **scythe**. Colonists held the wooden handle in both hands and swung the long, straight blade back and forth to cut plant stems near the ground. The cradle scythe was developed later in the colonial era. It had four wooden bars parallel to the blade. The bars pushed the grain down in tidy rows, so it was easy to gather and tie up. Farmers later used long sticks to beat the grain. The grains fell off and could be collected and bagged. The bare stems were called straw. This was used as animal food or bedding. *This is a crib, which was used to dry ears of corn.*

To increase his portion, the miller sometimes cheated. One way he did this was to make a tricky **toll dish**. The miller used this bucket or scoop to measure out his own portion of grain before grinding it. The miller might make his toll dish just a little too large, or he might drill indentations in it to catch extra amounts of grain. English law stopped this practice by requiring all toll dishes to be a standard size. The miller had to get a local official to check his toll dishes before using them. Alternatively, the miller could build a square wooden frame around the millstones to trap grain and meal in the corners. A very sneaky miller might even add a small chute that diverted some of the meal away during grinding. If Deane took more than his share, his customers were free to set up mills for their own use and to allow their neighbors to use the mills for free. Deane would make a better living by treating his customers fairly.

Deane built his mill on a small river that ran through the village and down to Plymouth Harbor. This river ran faster as it tumbled downhill, so it provided just the right amount of energy to push a waterwheel. But very soon after he finished his mill, Deane died unexpectedly. Plymouth Colony elected John Jenney as its new miller. Jenney negotiated a powerful agreement with Plymouth's leaders. It guaranteed the right to run this mill "to him and his

The Jenney gristmill still stands in Plymouth, Massachusetts.

heirs forever." When Jenney died, his son became the miller. After almost fifty years of service to Plymouth Colony, the Jenney gristmill was sold to another family, who owned it well into the nineteenth century.

By the Rules

Gristmills were so important in colonial America that most colonial governments passed laws governing them. A Maryland law from 1704 stated that a miller had to find twelve men who would support his request to build a new mill. These men wrote letters swearing that the miller was trustworthy and could afford to run the gristmill. They sent their letters to the sheriff.

The sheriff represented England's government and its king or queen. Upon getting such a letter, he began an investigation. If everything looked good, the miller told the sheriff where he wanted to set up the mill. Usually someone else owned the land in question. The landowner could choose to set up his own mill or to grant the miller 20 acres (8 hectares) of land—half on either side of the stream. This gave him access to the water, rocks, and trees he needed to build and maintain the gristmill over time. The miller had two years to build the mill. If he finished on time, his family would be in control of the mill and land for the next eighty years.

Virginia had laws that protected landowners. The miller received only 1 acre (0.4 ha) across from the mill. To reduce competition, however, the law guaranteed that other mills would be spaced out along the stream. As in England, Virginia laws required that the miller's toll dish be monitored and imposed a fine on cheaters. A 1751 law set the miller's toll at one-eighth of any grains he handled. This was a high wage, but the miller had to do good work. He could be forced to pay his clients back if the grain was ground poorly.

THREE

A Tour of the Gristmill

The deep, pounding thump of the gristmill was one of many familiar sounds in a colonial community. The noise came from the gristmill's main power source: a large, spinning waterwheel or windmill. Carrying far across the landscape, the sound proved to the colonists that the miller was hard at work.

When they first stood outside the gristmill, colonial children might have been confused. How could a waterwheel or windmill grind grain? The answer was hidden inside the mill building. The giant wheel provided energy to move the millstones. The miller supervised one of the most advanced industries in colonial America.

It's All Connected

The waterwheel or windmill outside the gristmill was only the first in a series of mechanical parts that moved the millstones. At the center of this wheel was a heavy wooden shaft that extended through the wall of the gristmill. The shaft was connected to a smaller, wooden wheel called the counterwheel. The counterwheel was actually a **gear**, with peglike teeth around its edges. Rising from the floor next to the counterwheel was a second, vertical shaft. It bore a smaller, horizontal gear whose teeth connected with the counterwheel. The vertical shaft connected to the top millstone. As in a quern, one stone sat on top of the other. But these millstones were much larger—as much as 7 feet (2 meters) in diameter. The bottom **bedstone** was attached to the floor of the mill. The shaft was mounted to the top stone, called the **runner stone**, with iron brackets.

The big outside wheel turned the counterwheel, which spun the second gear. The second gear rotated the vertical shaft and set the runner stone in motion. The size of each wheel played an important role in the system. A single turn of the outside wheel caused the smaller counterwheel to turn several times. These rapid turns of the smaller counterwheel allowed the millstones to grind a lot of grain quickly.

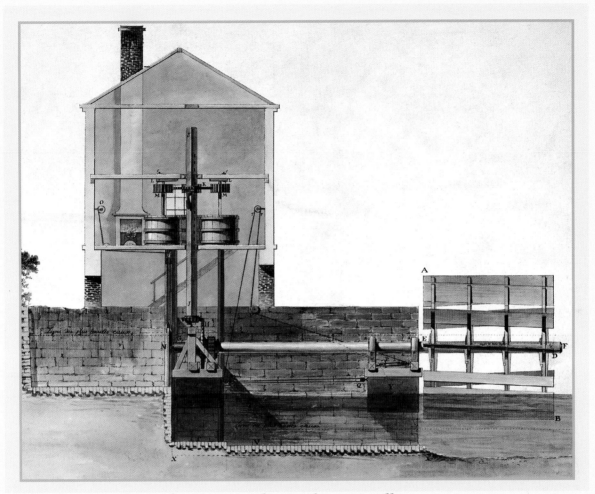

This diagram shows the inner workings of a gristmill.

Millstones were more costly than any other single part of the gristmill. They were usually made from high-quality granite or sandstone. These rough-textured rocks were good for grinding grains and also durable enough to last for years despite the constant motion. Millstones were sometimes found in the colonies. The

Ancient Technology

A gristmill is a complex structure with ancient roots. The Roman engineer Vitruvius described a water-powered gristmill in the first century BCE. In his time Romans preferred mills powered by animals or slaves. But by the fourth century CE, waterwheels could be found in Roman settlements across Europe. A historical land survey of England conducted in the year 1086 recorded 5,624 gristmills. Most of these probably ran on waterpower. Chinese engineer Tu Shih invented a waterwheel in 31 CE. It lay flat in the water and had a shaft that pointed upward. The counterwheel connected to levers that pulled bellows, which blew air onto blacksmiths' fires. Within a century, people had adopted similar horizontal waterwheels in Chinese gristmills as well.

Windmills originated in Iran more than a thousand years ago. These horizontal windmills were placed in windowed rooms atop stone gristmill towers. Their wood-and-fabric sails caught the wind and spun shafts attached to millstones below. Early European traders may have seen these windmills and brought information about their construction back home.

very best stones came from France, though the miller paid more for these stones and had to wait a long time to receive them.

Let It Flow

Although the miller sometimes had an expert millwright to help build his gristmill, it was his own knowledge that just as often got the job done. A water-powered mill could be built on almost any stream with a constant source of water. But the miller had to understand what type of wheel worked best in the water source that was available to him. If his mill was near a stream that always flowed swiftly, the miller might build an undershot wheel. This wheel had flat, wooden paddles arranged perpendicular to its rim. The water pushed against the paddles and caused the wheel to spin.

If he lived near a slower river or one that dried up seasonally, the miller often preferred an overshot wheel. This was a more powerful type of wheel, but its construction was also more complicated. First, the miller dammed the river to form a millpond upstream. He installed the wheel in a narrow wheel pit next to the mill building. The edges of the overshot wheel contained rows of overlapping wooden planks that formed V-shaped troughs. The miller dug a narrow channel called a raceway to carry

This overshot wheel runs on water power.

water from the millpond toward the waterwheel. He controlled the speed of water moving through the raceway by raising or lowering a **sluice gate**. Water poured onto the wheel from an artificial waterfall just above it. The troughs along the edges of the wheel then filled with water, and their weight made the wheel spin. The raceway continued beyond the wheel pit and carried water back to the main river channel.

Blowing in the Wind

Colonists sometimes used windmills to power gristmills near the coast, especially where the land was flat and winds blew steadily. A windmill usually had four long, narrow arms arranged in an X formation. Each arm was 20 feet (6 meters) or greater in length. It consisted of a gridlike wooden frame with a cloth cover. The arms attached to a central shaft, which ran into the top of the mill house and connected to the gear system.

A post windmill looked like a two-story wooden house perched atop a wooden stand. A large pole with a wheel at the end extended from one side of the building. Whenever the wind

A post windmill is able to turn in order to face the wind.

changed, the miller pushed this pole or tied up his horse to do the work for him. The entire house spun on the pole's base. He stopped when the arms faced into the wind, a position that made them spin most effectively.

A cap windmill was built of stone. Its base did not move. Instead, a wooden frame at the top of the building contained the arms. The miller used a pole to rotate this cap.

The miller had to pay special attention to wind speed. The arms did not begin to turn until the wind speed reached about 10 miles (16 kilometers) per hour. In fast winds he might have to roll up the cloth covers, called sails, to prevent wind damage. When necessary, he applied a brake on the windmill shaft to stop the arms from spinning. He always hoped for a moderate wind that provided steady power. The miller knew the weather could change at any time, so he never ignored a good wind—even if it meant working through the night.

FOUR

Running the Mill

Colonial craftsmen such as millers typically learned their skills during an **apprenticeship**. This was an on-the-job training period that began when a boy was eight to ten years old. Men from the community sometimes asked the miller to apprentice their sons. Among American colonists it was traditional for the eldest son to carry on his father's occupation. The miller's children often helped in the gristmill, and his oldest boy became an apprentice.

The apprentice wasn't paid for his work, but he was expected to do whatever he was told. Master craftsmen tolerated no laziness or misbehavior—even from their own sons. In return for a boy's hard work, the master taught him all the secrets of his craft. The miller not only showed his apprentice how to handle grains and to maintain the gristmill machinery but also passed on the skills needed to run a business. The apprentice studied reading, mathematics, and effective ways to deal with customers.

The miller had a variety of assistants, including apprentices and journeymen.

It could take up to seven years for an apprentice to complete his training. After that time he became a **journeyman**. He might be hired to work at an existing gristmill, or he could go in search of a place to start his own mill. The young miller could find a job at a plantation, especially if he lived in one of the southern colonies. Plantations were large farms that often had many workers and slaves. Whether the plantation owner grew grains or bought them, he needed a miller to provide flour for his community.

The journeyman could also become a merchant. A merchant miller set up shop in a large city such as Philadelphia, Boston, or New York. Farmers transported their grain to the city by boat or along the growing system of colonial roads. The merchant miller bought grain from them and made flour, which he exported to other colonies or countries. In good years, colonial farms produced enough grain for export to England and the West Indies' sugar plantations. A savvy merchant miller made a healthy profit and could become a wealthy member of colonial society.

Turning Grain into Flour

When the miller arrived to start his day, his apprentice was often already at work. On cold days the apprentice chopped wood and started a fire in the gristmill's large fireplace. Part of his job was to keep this fire going throughout the day. The apprentice also swept the mill floors every day. Loose grain attracted pests and mildew, and flour dust was a fire hazard.

Soon after breakfast, colonists began to arrive. They brought sacks of grain in carts or on the backs of horses. The miller and his apprentice helped them unload and then used a pulley system to move the heavy bags to the upper floors of the gristmill. Customers often waited while the miller ground their grain. This was a chance to talk to or to conduct business with neighbors. They might also barter with the miller's wife by trading grain for eggs, meat, or vegetables from her garden.

The miller began every job by cutting open the bags of grain. He measured his toll and set it aside, and then he put the remaining

Cook A Colonial Breakfast

Colonial millers ground large amounts of cornmeal, which was a staple of colonists' diet. People used cornmeal to make cornbread, hush puppies, pie crusts, and more. Another common recipe combined cornmeal, salt, and water to create a simple porridge. Settlers learned to cook it from Algonquin Indians, who called the dish suppawn. Virginians referred to it as hasty pudding because it was one of the few colonial foods that could be prepared quickly.

Colonists sometimes ate suppawn with gravy or vegetables at dinner. At breakfast or dessert, they added raisins and maple syrup or brown sugar. They also fried suppawn to make johnnycakes, which are similar to pancakes. Travelers and hunters carried cornmeal and salt in their bags. They needed only to boil water over a campfire for a quick meal any time of the day.

Suppawn makes a fun alternative to your morning oatmeal. But unlike colonists, we're used to food that cooks quickly. Suppawn takes more than half an hour to prepare, so try it on a weekend. Ask an adult to supervise as you work at the stove.

You Will Need

- medium saucepan with fitted lid
- mixing bowl
- pot holder
- timer
- wooden mixing spoon
- measuring cup (1- or 2-cup volume)
- set of measuring spoons
- cereal bowls
- cereal spoons
- water
- 1/3 cup yellow cornmeal
- 1/2 teaspoon salt
- maple syrup, brown sugar, raisins, or other favorite toppings
- milk or butter (optional)

Instructions

1. Measure 1/3 cup cornmeal. Pour into the mixing bowl.

2. Measure 1/2 cup water. Slowly stir into the mixing bowl until all of the cornmeal is wet.

3. Add 2 cups of water to the saucepan. Place the saucepan on the stove over medium heat.

4. When the water reaches a full boil, add 1/2 teaspoon salt.

5. Slowly stir in the damp cornmeal and place the lid on the pan.

6. Allow the mixture to simmer for about 30 minutes, stirring gently as often as you can. Don't allow the suppawn to stick to the bottom of the pan! The suppawn is ready when it is thick like oatmeal. Cooking times may vary, depending on your pot and stove.

7. Let the suppawn cool briefly before spooning it into individual bowls. Add raisins, maple syrup, or brown sugar. You may also enjoy a little milk or butter on top.

Bags of grain are what kept the miller busy every day. It was his job to transform the grain into flour.

grain into a wooden **hopper**. The hopper was shaped like an upside-down pyramid, with an open bottom that funneled into a chute. Grain fell steadily from the chute into a hole at the center of the runner stone.

An interesting feature of the millstones was the pattern of grooves cut into their surfaces. Grains cracked open when they were forced against the sharp corners of these grooves. The broken pieces of grain were rubbed between the stones, and powdery flour formed. Flour fell into the grooves and slowly moved toward the edges of the millstones, where it dropped to the bottom of the wooden frame surrounding them. Another chute led to a collecting bin, where the miller bagged the finished flour for the customer.

Every Detail Matters

The miller might have had many customers in a single day, but he could not grind every batch of grain the same way. Corn and wheat, barley and rye, oats and buckwheat—each grain had a different size and hardness. By turning a simple screw, the miller could adjust the space between his millstones to accommodate each grain. His goal was to make the finest possible flour or meal, which would cook with the best flavor and texture. To accomplish this, the miller sometimes set the stones so close together that a piece of paper could barely fit between them. But he had to be careful. Too much friction between the stones created heat and pressure. This released moisture in the grains, and the flour might rot. The miller tested the flour by running it through his fingers. If it was damp or clumpy, the stones were too close together. In that case, the miller raised the runner stone just a bit to allow more airflow. Apprentices learned to make these adjustments accurately through years of observation and practice.

The Other Workers

The miller and his apprentices or journeymen were not the only people who worked at the mill. Indentured servants and slaves also became part of the crew. The miller trained these workers at various tasks in the mill. He might even leave the gristmill to do other business while slaves or indentured servants kept it running.

An indentured servant was an English or European settler who could not afford their own fare to the colonies. A wealthier colonist such as the miller paid the fare. In return, he got several years of service from the person. Some of these people chose to travel to the colonies because they hoped for a new start. Others were taken from prisons or poorhouses and sold to ship captains. After arriving in the colonies, their indenture was sold to landowners.

Slave dealers bought slaves in Africa or the West Indies and sold them in the

Some millers kept slaves, who were required to work for no reward.

colonies. Slaves were required to work long hours and could be called on at any time. Most servants and slaves did not get to eat enough good food, and they didn't get good health care. They also usually lived in poor housing and suffered physical abuse if the owner believed they were not working hard enough.

Indentured servants and slaves often did similar jobs in the gristmill. They all suffered hardships. But there was one big difference in their lives. An indentured servant could expect to be freed after a period of years. Slaves, on the other hand, were considered property and could never expect to be free. The colonies did well because both of these groups did so much of the work.

The miller also had to be careful of fire. He listened for grinding sounds, which meant that the millstones were rubbing together. Friction could create sparks, which could cause the dusty flour or the wooden parts of the mill to catch fire. The gristmill's many gears, shafts, and pulleys also made telltale noises when they were not working well. Even the slightest odd sound or bit of smoke caused the miller to stop his work and look for the problem. The apprentice learned to keep the gears well oiled to prevent mechanical failures.

This miller is dressing the stones in his gristmill. Dressing the stones cleared out excess flour.

Dressing was another important task to be done at the gristmill. After a couple weeks of steady use, the grooves on the millstones became clogged with flour. The mill shut down completely for several days while the stones were cleaned. The first step in dressing the stones was to lift the runner completely off the bedstone. This was no small task, for the runner might weigh more than 2,000 pounds (900 kilograms). Huge hooks were inserted in the sides of the stone, and a pulley system raised the runner. The runner was gently turned over and laid on the floor with the grooves facing up. The miller or a hired expert, called the dresser, carefully chipped at the grooves of both stones until they were clean. While they were at it, they purposely scraped the spaces between grooves to roughen them. Then they remounted the runner, and the mill was once again ready to work for the community.

New Territory

The eighteenth century brought changes for the miller and his community. A tiny group of 144 Englishmen had settled Jamestown in 1607. By 1776, the colonial population had exploded to more than 2.5 million. All of these people needed food, and they were just as eager for land on which to grow it. In the early 1760s, colonists helped England fight French troops and their American

Indian allies for ownership of land west of the colonies. Upon winning the French and Indian War, England took control of rich farmland in the Ohio and Mississippi river valleys. Colonists were eager to begin settling the land they had fought to gain, but English leaders would not allow it.

This and other problems frustrated many colonists. The American Revolution began when more people wanted independence and access to more land. In 1783, King George III of England

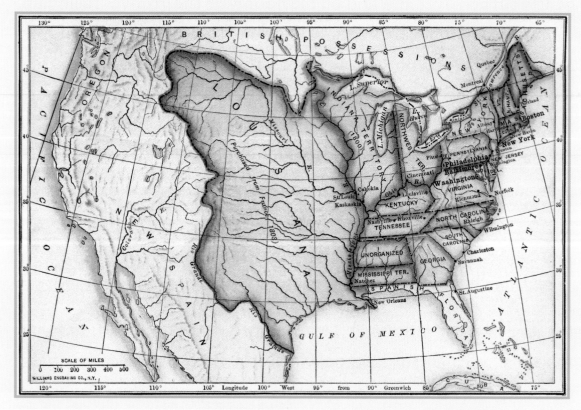

A map showing the territory gained from of the Louisiana Purchase.

recognized the United States of America as a separate nation. Between 1789 and 1794, three armies were sent to conquer the American Indian tribes of the Ohio Valley, and Americans could finally establish farms on this rich soil.

A decade later, a second expanse of land became available when President Thomas Jefferson purchased the Louisiana Territory from France. Stretching from the Mississippi River to the Rocky Mountains, the new territory included some of the best agricultural land in the nation. Once again, the U.S. government sent an army to conquer the American Indians. The Indians who survived were moved onto reservations. In the process the miller and farmer became partners in the settlement of another American breadbasket. Together they helped feed the growing nation as it pushed westward.

Glossary

apprenticeship	an agreement by which a person works with an expert to learn a new skill or job
bedstone	the lower, stationary millstone of a mill
bushel	a basket or other container with a capacity of 8 gallons (30 liters)
craftsmen	trained workers who make objects by hand
cribs	raised wooden boxes in which grain is stored
dressing	cleaning millstones to remove accumulated flour
exported	sold to other countries
gear	a toothed wheel that interlocks with a similar part to transmit motion through a mechanical system
grains	the seeds of various food plants
gristmill	a mill for grinding grain
hopper	a container that funnels grain toward millstones
journeyman	a craftsman who has completed his apprenticeship
meal	corn or other grain that has been ground to a powder
millwright	a craftsman who designed and built water mills or windmills
mortar	a hollowed-out object in which grains are pounded to make flour or meal
overshot wheel	a waterwheel onto which water pours from above
pestle	an object used to pound grain in a mortar
pottle	a drinking bowl with a set volume of 2 quarts (1.9 liters)
quern	a simple mill in which the user turns a handle on the top millstone to grind grain

raceway	a man-made channel of water that flows toward an overshot waterwheel
runner stone	the upper stone of a mill
scythe	a long-handled blade used for cutting grains
sluice gate	a board that can be raised or lowered to control the flow of water on the raceway of a mill
suppawn	an Algonquin Indian porridge made from cornmeal
toll	the portion of grain that a miller took as payment
toll dish	a dish or bowl for measuring the toll in mills
undershot wheel	a waterwheel that spins as water pushes its paddles from below

Find Out More

BOOKS

Cooper, Michael L. *Jamestown, 1607*. New York: Holiday House, 2007.

Kalman, Bobbie. *A Visual Dictionary of a Colonial Community*. New York: Crabtree Publishing Company, 2008.

Roberts, Russell. *Life in Colonial America*. Hockessin, DE: Mitchell Lane Publishers, 2007.

Winters, Kay. *Colonial Voices: Hear Them Speak*. New York: Dutton Juvenile, 2008.

WEBSITES

Colonial Williamsburg Kids Zone

www.history.org/kids/

Tour the colonial capital of Virginia and meet some of its important residents. This site contains games, activities, and many resources about colonial life and history.

George Washington's Mount Vernon

www.mountvernon.org/learn/explore_mv/index.cfm/ss/31/

Explore the first president's Virginia plantation, including his gristmill, farms, and mansion.

The Jenney Grist Mill

www.jenneygristmill.org/history.asp

Learn the history of one of America's oldest gristmills, built in 1636 by settlers at Plymouth.

Jump Back in Time: Colonial America (from the Library of Congress)

www.americaslibrary.gov/jb/colonial/jb_colonial_subj.html

Read stories from the history of Colonial America.

Robertson's Windmill

www.history.org/Almanack/life/trades/trademil.cfm

Take a look at the replica of the post windmill that served Colonial Williamsburg in the 1700s.

Index

Page numbers in **boldface** are illustrations.

About the Author

Christine Petersen has written more than three dozen books and several magazine articles for a variety of audiences, from emerging readers to adults. Her subjects include science, nature, and social studies. When she's not writing, Petersen and her young son enjoy exploring the natural areas near their home in Minneapolis, Minnesota. Petersen is a member of the Society of Children's Book Writers and Illustrators.